STAR FACTORIES

THE BIRTH OF STARS AND PLANETS

Ray Jayawardhana

RAINTREE
STECK-VAUGHN
PUBLISHERS

A Harcourt Company

Austin · New York
www.steck-vaughn.com

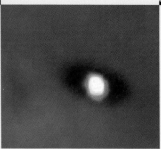

**In loving memory of
Dr. Somapala Jayawardhana,
my father and my hero**

Steck-Vaughn Company

First published 2001 by Raintree Steck-Vaughn Publishers,
an imprint of Steck-Vaughn Company.

Copyright © 2001 Turnstone Publishing Group, Inc.
Copyright © 2001, text, by Ray Jayawardhana.

Library of Congress Cataloging-in-Publication Data

Jayawardhana, Ray
     Star factories : the birth of stars and planets / Ray Jayawardhana.
        p.   cm. — (Space explorer)
     Includes bibliographical references and index.
     Summary: Examines the formation and evolution of stars and discusses how astronomers
study this process.
     ISBN 0-7398-2212-8 (hardcover) ISBN 0-7398-2222-5 (softcover)
     1. Stars—Formation—Juvenile literature. 2. Planets—Origin—Juvenile literature.
[1. Stars—Formation.] I. Title. II. Series.
QB806 .J39 2000
523.8'8—dc21   00-021703
                                                                        CIP

For information about this and other Turnstone reference books and educational materials, visit
Turnstone Publishing Group on the World Wide Web at http://www.turnstonepub.com.

Photo credits listed on page 64 constitute part of this copyright page.

Printed and bound in the United States of America.

1 2 3 4 5 6 7 8 9 0 LB 05 04 03 02 01 00

CONTENTS

HOLES IN THE HEAVENS

"I have looked further into space than any human being did before."— William Herschel

William Herschel climbed the ladder to his telescope and looked inside. He described what he saw. His younger sister Caroline sat at the foot of the ladder and recorded her brother's observations. Night after night for more than 20 years, the Herschels counted stars. William Herschel, who is best known for discovering the planet Uranus, wanted to find the shape of the Milky Way galaxy. To build a picture of the galaxy, he mapped large areas of the sky. To do this he recorded the location and brightness of stars.

Today, astronomers use cameras attached to telescopes to map the sky. But the Herschels lived more than 200 years ago, before the invention of photography in 1839. So together they became a kind of human camera. William Herschel described each star he saw while Caroline Herschel carefully wrote down his descriptions. The process was slow and difficult, but in time they mapped the position and brightness of more than 90,000 stars.

The Herschels noticed that in some parts of the sky there were no stars. William Herschel called these areas "holes in the heavens." These holes were an unsolved mystery for more than 100 years.

(above)
William Herschel and Caroline, his sister, were born in the mid-1700s in what is now Germany. They later moved to England, where they became astronomers. In 1781 William Herschel discovered the planet Uranus. Caroline Herschel was also an accomplished astronomer. She discovered eight comets.

(left)
The Herschels sometimes found places in the sky where they could see no stars. They called these "holes in the heavens." This picture shows a similar "hole," called Barnard 68. It was photographed in April 1999 in the sky above the Southern Hemisphere.

In Focus

Sir Isaac Newton invented the reflecting telescope in 1670. Many amateur stargazers use reflecting telescopes, like the one at right, today. Here is how it works.

Light enters a tube at one end and travels to a mirror at the other end. That mirror is shaped like a parabola. A parabola has a special property. It focuses light to a point. In this case, light that travels parallel to the sides of the telescope's tube is reflected by the parabolic mirror to a single point, called the focus. (See the picture at right.)

Before the light reaches the focus, it strikes a flat mirror, placed at an angle. From there, the light is reflected again, to a hole at the side of the telescope.

A star watcher simply looks in this hole through an eyepiece. The eyepiece then magnifies the image, making it appear larger.

In 1789 William Herschel built a similar reflecting telescope, shown at left.

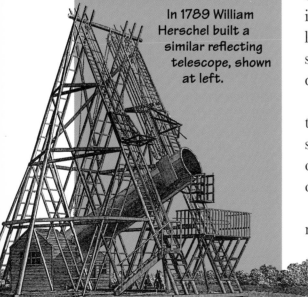

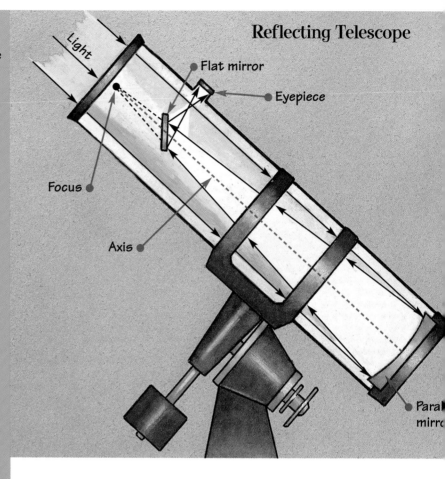

Reflecting Telescope

Light

Flat mirror

Eyepiece

Focus

Axis

Para
mirr

The dark "holes" Herschel had described became better understood in the early 1900s, thanks to the work of astronomer E. E. Barnard. Barnard was photographing bright shapes in the sky called nebulae (NEH-byoo-lee). He realized that these bright nebulae were the same shape as the dark "holes" William Herschel had described. Were they alike in other ways?

In 1923 astronomer Max Wolf suggested that both the dark shapes and the bright shapes were made of the same materials, dust and gas. Some of these nebulae, or clouds, appear bright because light from stars inside the clouds is reflected back toward Earth.

During the 1950s astronomers learned more about nebulae. They mapped the Northern Hemisphere sky,

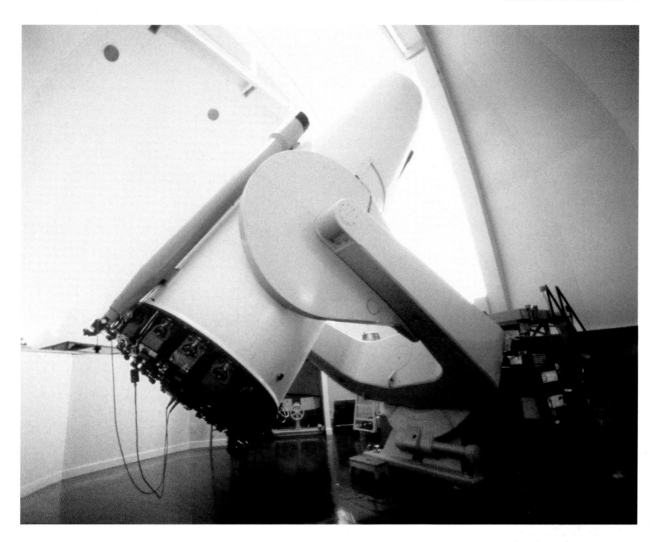

just as William and Caroline Herschel had done in the 1800s. These astronomers used a telescope on Mount Palomar in California to photograph the part of the sky that could be seen from that location. They counted about 1,800 nebulae in their photographs.

By now, astronomers have mapped nebulae in both hemispheres. In all, astronomers have found almost 3,000 nebulae in the sky. Astronomers like me are fascinated by these clouds. We have a theory that nebulae are where stars are formed. It is possible that nebulae are the star factories of our universe.

Larger parabolic mirrors inside telescopes make it possible to detect dimmer sources of light. The 48-inch Ochin Telescope, located on Mount Palomar in California, has conducted two programs to photograph the entire northern sky. The first program ended in 1956, and the second in 2000. The photographs from these programs form two sky atlases used by researchers around the world.

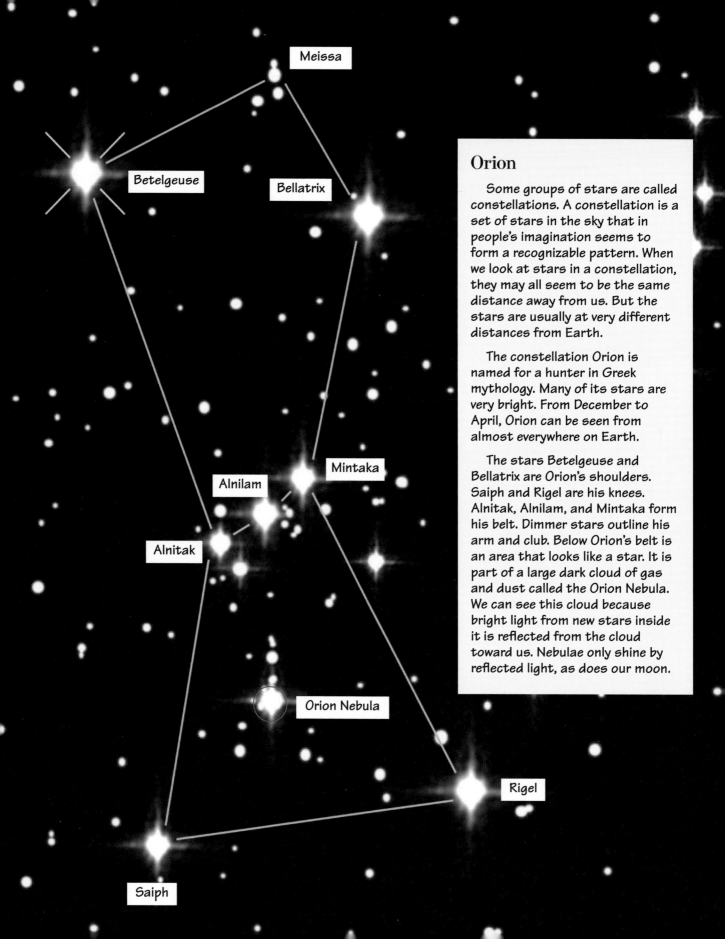

Meissa

Betelgeuse

Bellatrix

Mintaka

Alnilam

Alnitak

Orion Nebula

Rigel

Saiph

Orion

Some groups of stars are called constellations. A constellation is a set of stars in the sky that in people's imagination seems to form a recognizable pattern. When we look at stars in a constellation, they may all seem to be the same distance away from us. But the stars are usually at very different distances from Earth.

The constellation Orion is named for a hunter in Greek mythology. Many of its stars are very bright. From December to April, Orion can be seen from almost everywhere on Earth.

The stars Betelgeuse and Bellatrix are Orion's shoulders. Saiph and Rigel are his knees. Alnitak, Alnilam, and Mintaka form his belt. Dimmer stars outline his arm and club. Below Orion's belt is an area that looks like a star. It is part of a large dark cloud of gas and dust called the Orion Nebula. We can see this cloud because bright light from new stars inside it is reflected from the cloud toward us. Nebulae only shine by reflected light, as does our moon.

Looking Inside the Clouds

One nebula that interests many sky watchers is the Orion Nebula. It's possible to see this pretty formation by looking at the night sky with binoculars or a small telescope. Professional astronomers use their powerful telescopes to study the Orion Nebula, too. It may hold clues to the birth of our solar system and others like it.

Because there's no way we know to go back in time, astronomers cannot see how our sun and planet formed. However, we can find clues elsewhere to understand the origin, or beginning, of our solar system. One place astronomers look is the Orion Nebula. It is a star factory.

The part of the Orion Nebula we see shines with light from newborn stars that is reflected from the nebula. It is a good place for astronomers to learn what our own sun might have looked like a long time ago. It is one of the star factories nearest to Earth.

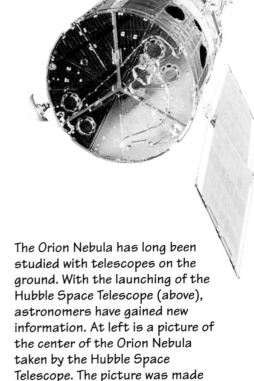

The Orion Nebula has long been studied with telescopes on the ground. With the launching of the Hubble Space Telescope (above), astronomers have gained new information. At left is a picture of the center of the Orion Nebula taken by the Hubble Space Telescope. The picture was made by combining 45 separate Hubble pictures.

Astronomically Big

The objects astronomers study are very large and usually far, far away. To describe them, astronomers have come up with their own units in which to express sizes, distances, and masses.

A standard unit of distance in astronomy is a light-year. That is the distance that light travels in one year. Light moves at a constant speed of about 300,000 kilometers (about 186,000 miles) per second. So a light-year is about 9 trillion kilometers (about 6 trillion miles). The sun is a little more than eight light-minutes, that is, around 150 million kilometers (about 93 million miles) from Earth. Starting from the sun, light takes about eight minutes to reach Earth. The Orion Nebula is about 1,500 light-years from Earth.

The amount of matter in stars and dark clouds is huge as well. Astronomers describe mass using the mass of the sun as a unit of measurement. One solar mass is about two thousand billion billion billion ("2" followed by 30 zeroes) kilograms (about four thousand billion billion billion pounds).

The Orion Nebula is very large, but it is actually part of a much bigger cloud of gas and dust called a "giant molecular cloud." The mass of a giant cloud, that is, the amount of material inside it, can be as much as ten million times that of our sun. Giant clouds can also stretch for hundreds of light-years. A light-year is the distance that light travels in one year.

Giant clouds are made of about 99 percent gas and 1 percent dust. Most of the gas is hydrogen. There are also small amounts of carbon monoxide, water, ammonia, and other molecules. Most of the dust in the clouds is like the dust in the air on Earth. But scientists think that most of the particles are much tinier. New stars are made from the gas and dust found in giant clouds.

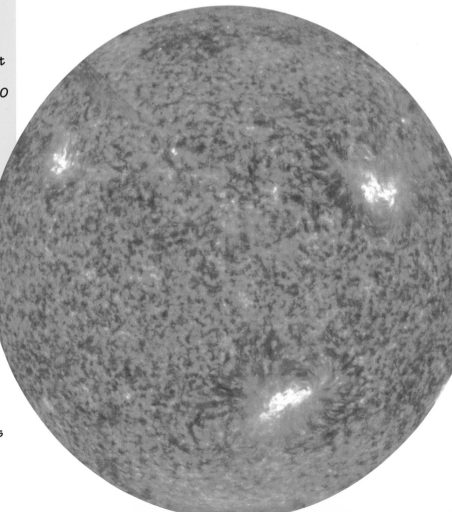

The mass of the sun (right) is 332,800 times the mass of Earth.

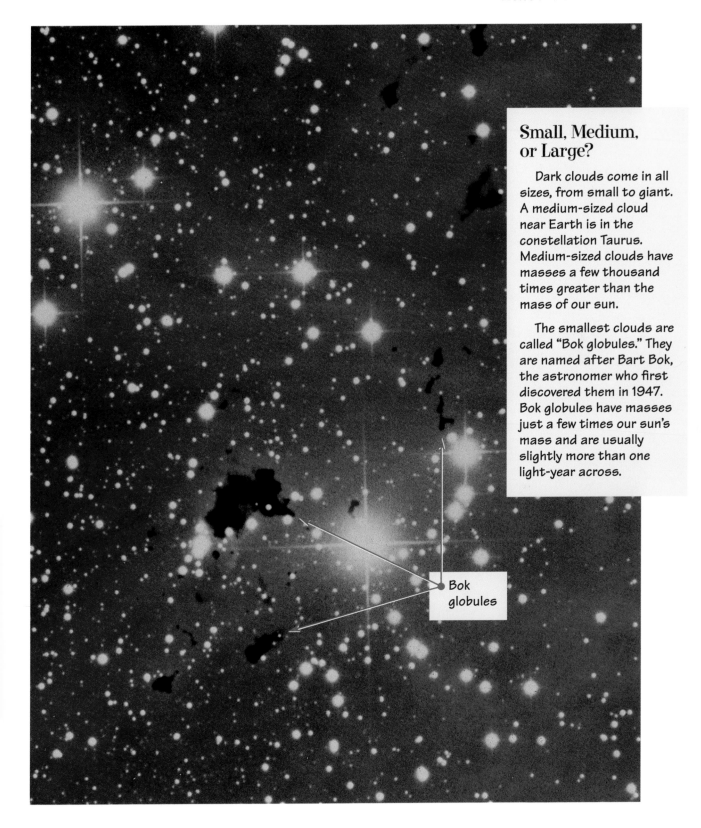

Small, Medium, or Large?

Dark clouds come in all sizes, from small to giant. A medium-sized cloud near Earth is in the constellation Taurus. Medium-sized clouds have masses a few thousand times greater than the mass of our sun.

The smallest clouds are called "Bok globules." They are named after Bart Bok, the astronomer who first discovered them in 1947. Bok globules have masses just a few times our sun's mass and are usually slightly more than one light-year across.

Bok globules

2

STAR FACTORIES IN THE CLOUDS

"We're looking at things that we think are very comparable to what our sun would have looked like when it was forming."—Elizabeth Lada

No one can watch the birth of a star. This process takes too long, probably hundreds of thousands of years. But scientists have developed a model to explain how stars are born. This model is based on observations of newborn stars. It follows the laws of physics.

The laws of physics are not really laws. People can't create a rule and expect nature to follow it. The laws of physics are models. They are based on observations of nature's behavior. One purpose of a model is to predict future outcomes. When a new observation contradicts, or goes against, a model, the model must be changed. We call certain models "laws" when nature seems to always behave according to predictions based on these laws. These laws seem to hold true everywhere on Earth and also everywhere in the universe.

To study stars, astronomers need a model of how light behaves, and how it moves. Light is very mysterious. The more scientists study its behavior, the more mysterious it seems. But some of its properties can be modelled fairly simply. These models are useful in predicting light's behavior under many circumstances.

One property of light concerns how it moves from place to place. Light often seems to travel in straight lines. Therefore, scientists created a model of light made of "rays" that trace the straight path light takes.

(above)
The hottest part of a flame is blue, a cooler part is orange, and the coolest part is red. Scientists combine observations of this pattern with the model of light as waves to form a "law of physics." The law states that the higher an object's temperature, the shorter the wavelengths of most light the object emits, or gives off. Blue light has shorter wavelengths than orange light, and orange light has shorter wavelengths than red light.

(left)
The description above likely holds true for objects in space, too. Stars with different colors, and so different surface temperatures, can be seen in this image from the Hubble Space Telescope.

Wave Model of Light

According to the wave model of light, light can have any wavelength from near zero to near infinity. Light that has practically all wavelengths is produced by many processes in nature. Depending on the process, more or less light will be produced in any given range of wavelengths.

For example, we cannot see very cold objects, like dark clouds, because most of the light they emit has long wavelengths, called radio waves, which we cannot see. Warmer objects, such as the human body, emit light with shorter wavelengths, called infrared light. The hottest processes in the universe mostly emit X-rays and gamma rays.

The chart below shows the names used for light of different wavelengths. Light with the shortest wavelengths is called gamma rays. Light with the longest wavelengths is called radio waves.

Some of light's behavior is better described with a different model. The light we see, called the visible spectrum, can be measured in waves. These waves have different lengths. A rainbow shows visible light separated into colors—red, orange, yellow, green, blue, indigo, violet. The wave model of light describes each color with a wave of different length. The length of these waves decreases from red to blue. Red light has a longer wavelength than blue light.

When we talk about light in this book, we use the wave model of light. The model gives us one way to describe some of light's behavior.

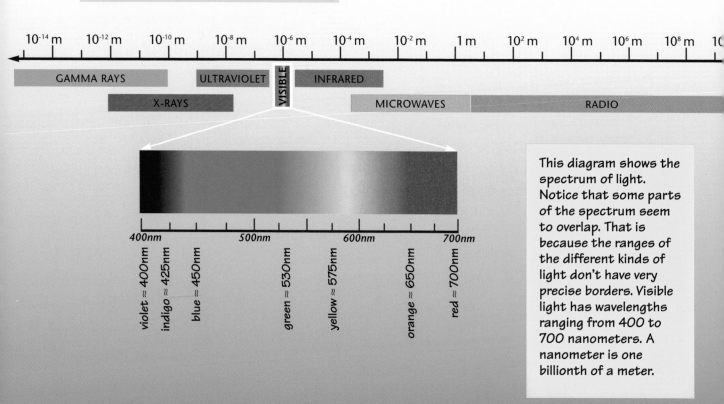

This diagram shows the spectrum of light. Notice that some parts of the spectrum seem to overlap. That is because the ranges of the different kinds of light don't have very precise borders. Visible light has wavelengths ranging from 400 to 700 nanometers. A nanometer is one billionth of a meter.

Light from Newborn Stars

We can't see most newborn stars because they are in the middle of clouds of gas and dust. The visible light from a newborn star is usually absorbed by the dust around it. So most new stars are invisible to telescopes that detect visible light. But there are other ways to see a new star. The light from a star inside a cloud warms the dust around it. The dust then emits infrared light. Our eyes are not very sensitive to infrared light. But we can build telescopes that are sensitive to this light.

William Herschel discovered infrared light in 1800. Since then, scientists have discovered light with both longer and shorter wavelengths than the light we can see with our eyes. All of these different wavelengths make up what scientists call the spectrum of light. Astronomers have now developed instruments that can detect most types of light. Instruments that detect infrared light are used to look inside star factories.

Discovering Invisible Light

William Herschel conducted an experiment and found that the different colors of light from the sun had different temperatures.

Herschel used an angled piece of glass called a prism, such as the one shown in the photograph, to separate the light from the sun into the colors of a rainbow. He also used a thermometer to measure each color's temperature. When he placed the thermometer just past the red part of the spectrum, he noticed that the temperature was higher than when no light passed through the prism. Something must have caused that increase in temperature.

Herschel had discovered what is now called infrared light. His experiment marked the first time anyone had found evidence for light we can't see with our eyes.

Seeing the Light

Astronomers use different kinds of telescopes to see light of different wavelengths. Some of the telescopes are on Earth and some are in space.

The pictures on these pages show Orion and the Orion Nebula in the light that each telescope was designed to record. Each picture is shown on a very different scale.

Gamma rays from the Orion Nebula were recorded in this picture made using the Imaging Compton Telescope. The telescope is part of the Compton Gamma-Ray Observatory (left), which was launched into space in 1991.

The Ultraviolet Imaging Telescope detected **Ultraviolet light**. This telescope was part of the Astro 2 Observatory (below) which was flown aboard the Space Shuttle *Endeavor*. The telescope made this picture of the Orion Nebula.

gamma rays

ultraviolet

VISIBLE

x-rays

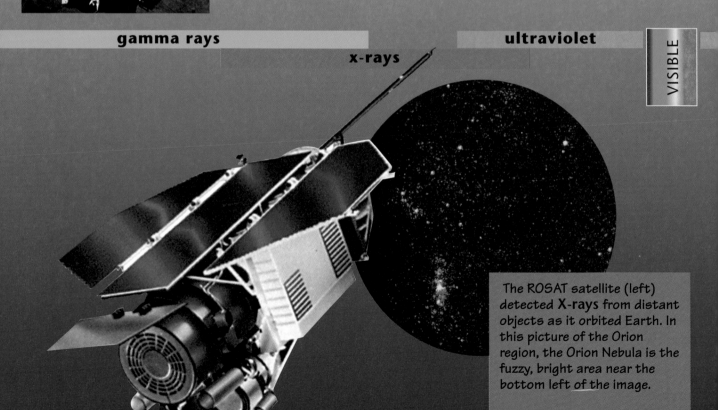

The ROSAT satellite (left) detected X-rays from distant objects as it orbited Earth. In this picture of the Orion region, the Orion Nebula is the fuzzy, bright area near the bottom left of the image.

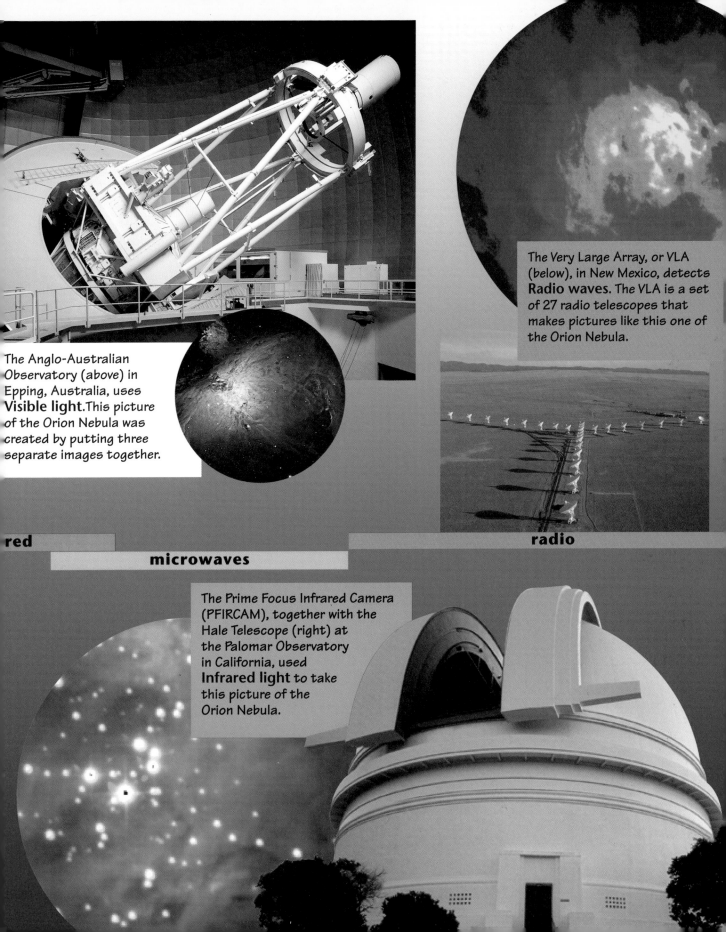

The Very Large Array, or VLA (below), in New Mexico, detects **Radio waves**. The VLA is a set of 27 radio telescopes that makes pictures like this one of the Orion Nebula.

The Anglo-Australian Observatory (above) in Epping, Australia, uses **Visible light**. This picture of the Orion Nebula was created by putting three separate images together.

red

radio

microwaves

The Prime Focus Infrared Camera (PFIRCAM), together with the Hale Telescope (right) at the Palomar Observatory in California, used **Infrared light** to take this picture of the Orion Nebula.

Making a Model

Understanding a process in nature, like the formation of stars, requires a model of that process. Here's an example of how a model is developed.

A Star Is Born

Astronomers study light that comes from star factories. They gather information that other astronomers use to develop a model of how stars are born. Here's how the birth of stars may happen.

The clouds are spread over very large regions, and they have very low densities. Density is mass per unit of volume, or the amount of matter in a certain quantity of space. The clouds have lots of space between molecules. In these clouds, there are far, far fewer molecules in a particular volume of space than in the same volume of air at Earth's surface. There may be as little as one molecule of gas or dust per cubic centimeter (about $\frac{1}{16}$ of a cubic inch) of a cloud.

Dark clouds spin slowly. Molecules of gas and dust inside the clouds bump around, just as they do in Earth's atmosphere. Deep inside these clouds, regions called cores form. Cores spin, just like the dark clouds that surround them. A core is the densest part of a cloud, but still far less dense than air.

Why does the core form? Astronomers believe that not all regions of these clouds start with the same density. According to scientists' models of nature's behavior, a part of a cloud with the highest density will grow. The

❶ Collect Evidence

Scientists observe how nature behaves. In this case, scientists gather the observations, or "snapshots," of star formation. They include pictures like these of a dark cloud (top left) and protostars (right). The pictures are made with data collected by telescopes on Earth and telescopes in space like IRAS (left).

part of a cloud that grows becomes the core. In time, the core has so much mass that it collapses, or shrinks, under its own weight. Its density is then very high.

The core spins faster as it shrinks. It begins to glow. This glowing mass is a baby star, or protostar. All of this happens in a few hundred thousand years. The average star lives about ten billion years. So the time it takes for a star to be born is short compared to its lifetime.

The details of the birth of a star are not clear to scientists. Astronomers can't watch the whole process with one star. So we collect "snapshots" of different stars at different stages in their lives. We apply our knowledge of the laws of physics to the snapshots to develop models of the star-birth processes. We use computers to put these snapshots together in different ways. We choose the model we think is best and make predictions based on the model. Then, we test these predictions by comparing them to information we gain from new observations.

➋ Use the Laws of Physics

Scientists think of conditions in nature that could have led to these "snapshots." They use the laws of physics and these conditions to make a model of star formation.

➌ Program the Computer

The scientist programs the computer to calculate the model's prediction of the various steps in star formation. To be a useful model, the prediction must agree with the "snapshot" observations.

Frank Shu, a professor at the University of California at Berkeley, studies star formation. In 1977 he proposed a model that describes how a core collapses and becomes a baby star.

Frank's model predicted that the center of a cloud core collapses faster than the outside of the core. Thus, a protostar probably forms in the middle of the core. The model predicted that gas and dust spin around the protostar and slowly fall inside.

Frank's model also predicted that the cloud of gas and dust spinning around the protostar would flatten into a disk shape. It would be like a ball of pizza dough flattening when someone spins it in the air. The disk would spin around the protostar.

Results from other models predict that as a new star contracts in size, it becomes hotter. When it is hot enough, powerful nuclear reactions, like those in a hydrogen bomb, begin. Nuclear reactions start when hydrogen atoms in the star combine to make helium atoms. This process releases huge amounts of light. We see this light from Earth. When a protostar emits visible light, it has become a true star. A star that is the size of our sun can shine for about ten billion years by making helium from hydrogen.

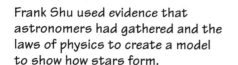

Frank Shu used evidence that astronomers had gathered and the laws of physics to create a model to show how stars form.

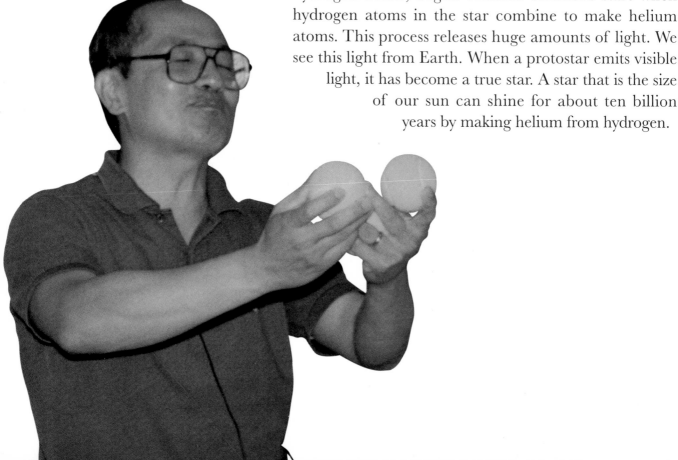

Core Hunting

The more astronomers learn about cores, the more they learn about the birth of stars. Astronomers can't see cores with traditional telescopes because the cores are hidden by dust. How do they find cores to study? In the early 1980s, astronomer Phil Myers (above) of the Harvard-Smithsonian Center for Astrophysics in Cambridge, Massachusetts, and fellow astronomer Priscilla Benson (right), now of Wellesley College in Wellesley, Massachusetts, used a radio telescope to try to find cores. A radio telescope can detect radio waves emitted by various molecules.

Priscilla and Phil looked for radio emissions from ammonia molecules. They chose ammonia because these molecules are found mostly in cloud cores. "We wanted to find out where in the clouds the cores were…. We also wanted to know if the cores were common and how long they lived," Phil explains. "Ammonia lets us zoom in on the dense parts of clouds to find the cores."

Since Phil and Priscilla began their work, astronomers have found hundreds of cores. Some of the cores seem to be shrinking, or collapsing. Inside those shrinking cores, stars will be born in a few hundred thousand years.

The arrows point to the same star in both pictures.

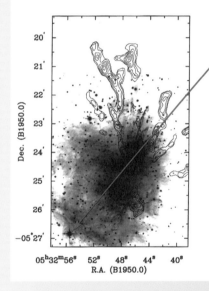

This picture is an infrared image of part of the Orion Nebula. A special filter was used to block all wavelengths except those in the infrared region. Just as in a print of a photograph, white areas in this picture show more intense emissions of light.

This is a picture of radio emissions from ammonia in part of the Orion Nebula laid on top of an infrared image. The contour lines of the radio emissions show the different intensities of radio waves emitted by the ammonia. The shaded areas show infrared emissions. In this picture, the darker the area, the more intense is the emitted light, just as in a negative of a photograph.

Birth of a Star

Astronomers use observations and the laws of physics to make models. Models explain processes in nature. The models scientists create fit the evidence that they have. If they collect new evidence that doesn't fit their models, scientists improve their models. The model on these pages offers a simple explanation of how stars may be born.

1 The gas and dust inside a cloud collect. They form a few protostars inside denser parts of the cloud.

2 Each protostar eventually becomes a star and produces its own light. Dust and gas outside the star flatten into a disk. Some material is ejected, or thrown out, from the star's poles.

3 Each disk is 20 to 50 times smaller than the original cloud. (These pictures are not drawn to the same scale.)

Infrared cameras were just becoming available at the time Elizabeth Lada began to study newborn stars in clouds. She knew that an infrared camera would be perfect for finding out more about where in the clouds stars form. Elizabeth's work showed that most stars in Orion are born in groups.

How do we know that this model's prediction describes nature's behavior? Astronomers have detected cloud cores that seem to be collapsing. We also have pictures of the late stages of a star's birth. Some snapshots are in radio light, and some are in visible light. Still others are in infrared light. Infrared light from a core could be a sign that protostars are on their way to becoming stars.

By the mid-1980s, astronomers like Charles Lada at the Harvard-Smithsonian Center for Astrophysics in Cambridge, Massachusetts, showed that many dark clouds contained infrared light. This infrared light suggested that baby stars were probably forming. But it didn't tell him exactly where the stars formed, or if there were many newborn stars inside the same cloud. Charles still had questions, and his sister, Elizabeth Lada, answered them.

Elizabeth used a telescope with an infrared camera to make a picture of a large part of the Orion cloud. The results were surprising. Elizabeth found that instead of being scattered throughout the cloud, most protostars are born in one of three large groups, or clusters. Each cluster has hundreds of stars.

Charles and Elizabeth Lada now work together with other astronomers to study several dark clouds. They keep finding what Elizabeth first found. Most stars are born within groups of hundreds or thousands of stars.

But the stars don't stay in these groups. Why? Based on their observations and models, scientists think that young stars produce powerful winds. These winds probably blow away most of the remaining gas. No longer massive enough to be bound by its own gravity, the group could then break up and the stars scatter in space.

Most protostars are born in a few large groups. This is one of Elizabeth Lada's infrared photographs of part of the Orion Nebula. The cluster of about 500 young stars she studies are within a dark, flame-shaped region of the Orion Nebula called the Flame Nebula.

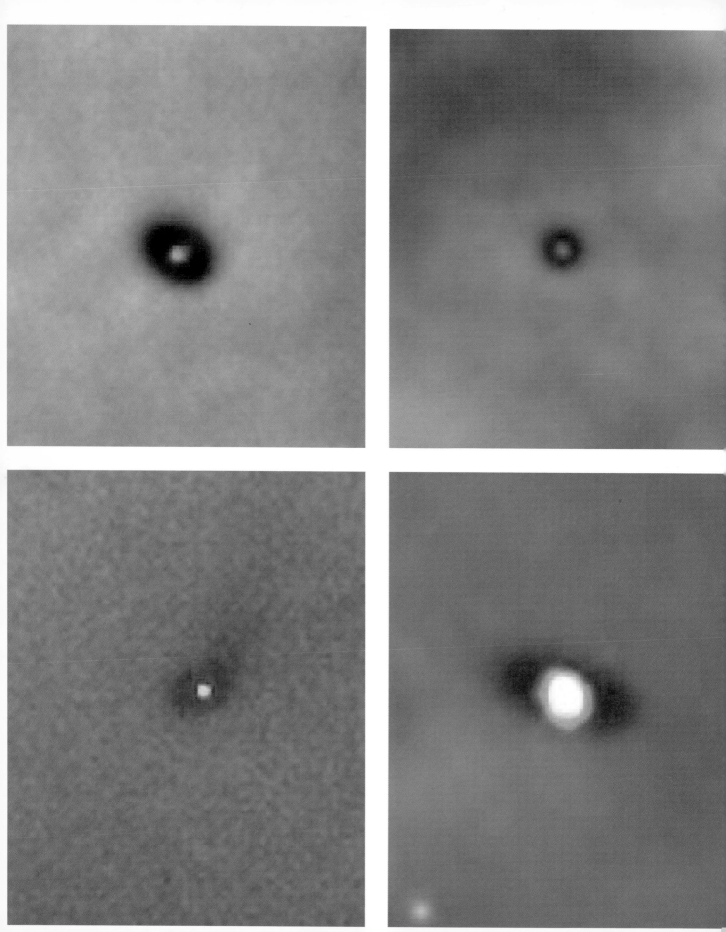

3

DUST DISKS UNCOVERED

"Seeing these disks ... makes us believe that the process of planetary formation may be fairly common."—Richard Terrile

(above)
The idea that planetary systems are born out of gas clouds isn't new. In 1755 Prussian philosopher and physicist Immanuel Kant suggested that our solar system formed in a clump of gas. He even suggested that the cloud would flatten into a disk. Almost 250 years later, astronomers continue work based on Kant's ideas.

(left)
These photographs of young disks in the Orion Nebula were taken by the Hubble Space Telescope between January 1994 and March 1995. These disks stand out against the bright gas of the Orion Nebula. The disks range in size from 1,300 to 5,200 light-minutes across.

When Frank Shu presented his model of the birth of the star, many parts of the process that his model predicted had never been seen. Did his model accurately describe these parts? In 1994 astronomers aimed the Hubble Space Telescope at the Orion Nebula and found part of the answer. They saw the first images of disks of dust and gas spinning around young stars. And there were not just a few disks. Almost half of the new stars in Orion, each barely a million years old, may be surrounded by disks. Many of the disks appear larger than our whole solar system. The Hubble Telescope gave astronomers another snapshot to help them understand how stars and planets form.

Even before the Hubble Space Telescope discovery, there was evidence of disks around young stars. Visible light from disks can't usually be seen from Earth. But astronomers have found clues in infrared light. Disks are only about one percent dust, but the infrared light emitted by that dust can be detected.

The dust in a disk absorbs light from the star inside the disk. The dust warms a little, and the warm dust glows at infrared wavelengths. Astronomers can detect the infrared emissions that come from the dust. A star with a disk looks brighter in infrared light than a similar star without a disk.

The Hubble Space Telescope took this infrared picture of a young star in the constellation Taurus. The dark, slanted region in the middle may be the edge of a disk. Small amounts of material above and below the disk reflect the star's light. We see these reflections as bright areas in the picture. Astronomers call this young star the "Butterfly Star." It is about 9,800 light-minutes across.

In the star factories that have been observed, at least half of all the one-million-year-old stars emit infrared light we can measure. That may mean that about half of all young stars have disks.

Another clue that disks exist comes from gas. A disk is 99 percent gas in mass. Radio telescopes can detect radio light emitted by several kinds of molecules that are usually part of the gas. Carbon monoxide is one kind of molecule that is easy to find.

The Hubble Space Telescope has now taken pictures in visible light of about two dozen young stars with disks. They are inside star factories in the constellations Orion and Taurus.

For many years, scientists had clues that dust disks existed. Now, with Hubble's images, astronomers know for certain that many young stars are circled by dust disks. Older stars don't have dust disks. Or their disks are much less dense. As a star ages, astronomers asked, where do the dust and gas go?

Many astronomers think that when stars are about ten million years old, the dust and gas in the disks begin to form planetary systems. Our solar system is a planetary system. It has planets that orbit, or move around, a star, our sun. Astronomers have found strong evidence to support their theory that planetary systems like ours come from dust and gas around a star.

One piece of evidence is in the mass of young stars' disks. Astronomers estimate that each such disk has more than ten times the mass that is needed to make a planetary system like ours.

In 1983 images from the Infrared Astronomy Satellite (IRAS) found another clue. The satellite found signs of dust around some grown-up stars. But disks around older stars had much less dust than disks around younger stars.

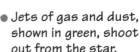

This Hubble Space Telescope picture shows a side view of the disk of HH30, a young star in the constellation Taurus. Because this disk is seen from the "side," it doesn't show the light of the star inside it. This makes the disk itself look like a dark line that widens at the edges. The disk, which is about 3,500 light-minutes across, shoots out jets of dust and gas.

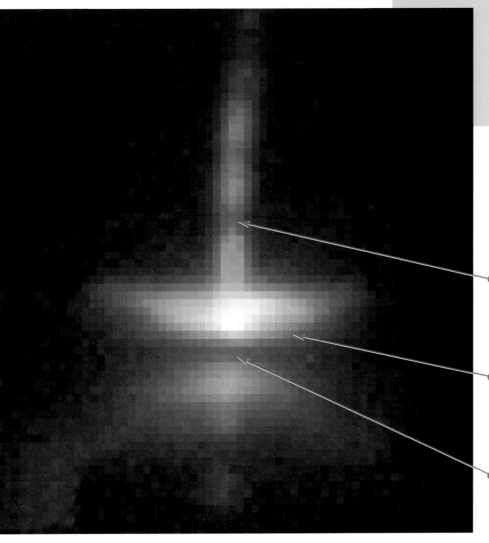

Jets of gas and dust, shown in green, shoot out from the star.

Light from the star can be seen only as it reflects off the top and the bottom of the disk.

The star is probably hidden in the disk. The disk is the slightly darkened horizontal band.

Star Children

Scientists believe that very soon after the universe began, there were only hydrogen, helium, and a few other elements. But we have carbon in our skin, iron in our blood, and calcium in our bones. Where did those elements come from? They were all made inside stars. We are made from star material.

Stars emit light when they change simple elements into more complex ones. They do this by a process called nuclear fusion. In nuclear fusion, smaller nuclei collide at very high speed and form a larger nucleus. Nuclei are the central parts of tiny particles of matter called atoms.

Most medium-sized stars like our sun shine because light is emitted during nuclear fusion as hydrogen atoms join to make helium atoms. Older, bigger stars also make other elements. When their helium atoms combine, carbon and oxygen form. Almost all elements in the universe were made through nuclear reactions.

When stars explode or their outer parts are blown away in strong winds, the elements they've made spread out into space. Because our solar system formed long after many stars had lived and died, the material that made our solar system was rich in those stars' ashes. So, we are truly the children of stars.

Many heavy atoms—like gold—are made only when huge stars explode in an event called a supernova.

The ashes of a star that exploded here in the N206 Nebula are shown in green.

Ashes from similar explosions slowly gather into clouds, shown in yellow and red. New stars are being born in these clouds.

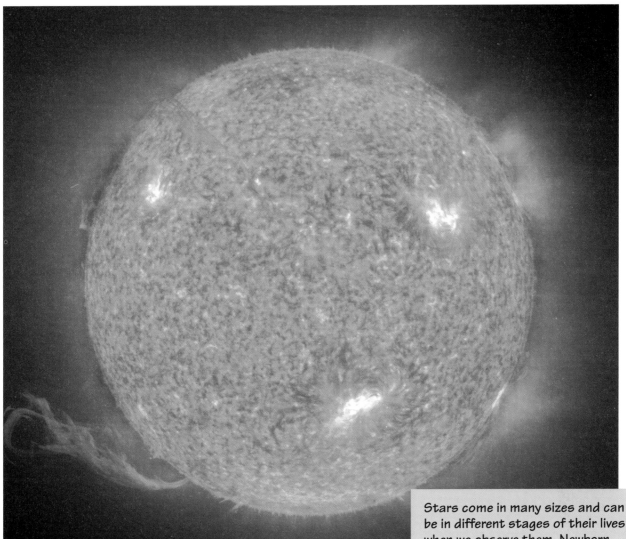

Disk Detectives

In 1983 two astronomers took a picture in visible light of the dust disk around one of the grown-up stars IRAS had observed. This picture represented quite an accomplishment. The light from a star inside a disk is so bright that it can be hard to see the much fainter light reflected by the disk. Astronomers Bradford Smith, then of the

Stars come in many sizes and can be in different stages of their lives when we observe them. Newborn stars, or protostars, are a few hundred thousand years old. Young stars may be between about one and two million years old. Adolescent, or teenage, stars may be tens of millions of years old. A star is called mature, or grown up, when it is about a hundred million years old. At about five billion years of age, the sun is considered a very mature star. This ultraviolet image of the sun was taken by the Solar and Heliospheric Observatory's Extreme-ultraviolet Imaging Telescope.

University of Arizona, and Richard Terrile of the Jet Propulsion Laboratory in California, used a device called a coronagraph to block the light from the star. They attached very thin silk threads to the edges of the coronagraph's lens. These threads suspended a tiny plastic disc over the middle part of the lens. The disc blocked out the star's light. The coronagraph could then make an image of the disk around Beta Pictoris, a 100-million-year-old star about 50 light-years away from Earth.

This picture was the first image of a disk around a mature, or grown-up, star. Unlike the Orion disks, the Beta Pictoris disk had only a small amount of gas and dust. Astronomers thought that the rest of the gas and dust may have become parts of planets. They wondered if Beta Pictoris is the sun for a group of planets. But it was too far away for astronomers to be sure. Brad and Rich had clues, but they could not see an orbiting planet.

Brad and Rich then used the coronagraph to look for disks around other stars. They studied mature stars nearby, but they found no disks. For 15 years, Beta Pictoris was the only mature star with a disk that astronomers had been able to photograph. That changed in 1998.

Brad Smith, right, and Rich Terrile are standing beside the 2.5-meter Dupont telescope at the Las Campanas Observatory in Chile. The coronagraph is inside the blue cylinder attached to the telescope.

The dust disk around this mature star, known as Beta Pictoris, may have a planetary system inside.

Part of the dust disk

Plastic disc placed on coronagraph lens to block light from Beta Pictoris

Part of the dust disk

Silk thread

Silk thread

4

OFF TO CHILE

"This is a big discovery. This is huge!"—Charles Telesco

When I was in college, I heard Charles Lada talk about his sister Elizabeth's discovery that stars are born in groups of hundreds or even thousands. This discovery interested me. I wanted to know more about how stars are born and change over time. I learned that new infrared instruments were helping astronomers study the birth of stars.

After college, I was so interested in stars that I continued my studies as a graduate student at the Harvard-Smithsonian Center for Astrophysics (called "the CfA"). There I found out more about how disks around young stars evolve. In Orion the young stars with disks are barely one million years old. Our sun is about five billion years old and has no disk. What happens to the disk? Like other astronomers, I wanted to know about a process that takes too long to observe. I needed snapshots of many stars at different stages of their growth to give me clues.

But there were no pictures of disks around adolescent, or teenage, stars. A star is an adolescent when it is about ten million years old. Astronomers think this is about the time when planets form. I wanted to know how ten-million-year-old disks are different from one-million-year-old disks. And I wanted to find signs of planets forming. I decided to try to take a picture of a disk around a teenage star.

(above)
The Cerro Tololo InterAmerican Observatory is on top of a mountain about 500 kilometers (about 300 miles) north of Santiago, Chile.

(left)
The observatory houses several telescopes, including the Victor M. Blanco telescope, shown in the middle. The ground in this photograph appears curved because the photographer used a fisheye lens. A fisheye lens records up to a 180-degree field of vision.

35

When I began my work on adolescent stars in 1998, 15 years had passed since the Infrared Astronomy Satellite (IRAS) first found signs of disks around mature stars. That was the first time astronomers took a picture of the disk around Beta Pictoris. Technology had improved since then. Infrared cameras had become much more sensitive. It was a good time to look for disks again.

To get a close look at the stars, scientists sometimes must travel a long way. In 1998 the largest telescope in the Southern Hemisphere was at the Cerro Tololo Inter-American Observatory (CTIO) in Chile. It sits 2,500 meters (about 8,000 feet) above sea level. Its parabolic mirror is 4 meters (about 13 feet) across.

The CTIO was built on a remote mountain for a good reason. It's a nearly perfect place to do astronomy. The mountain is far away from city lights, so the sky is dark. That makes it easier to see faint objects. The air is very dry, which is best for infrared observations because water vapor in the atmosphere absorbs infrared light. The more water vapor in the air, the less infrared light that reaches the telescope. And the sky above the observatory is clear most nights. It doesn't matter how dark the night is or how dry the air is if you can't see through the clouds!

Getting to use a big telescope like the one at CTIO isn't easy. Astronomers from around the world have to compete for time. Each year astronomers on a small CTIO committee read proposals from scientists. Then they choose what they think are the most interesting projects and assign time for scientists to use the telescope.

I sent a proposal telling the committee I wanted to take infrared pictures of ten-million-year-old stars. I made a list of stars I would observe. Most of the stars on my

Telescopes that see far into space are large, and so are the buildings that house them. The dome, or rounded top, of the Victor M. Blanco telescope is as tall as a four-story building. The dome can rotate to let the telescope point in different directions.

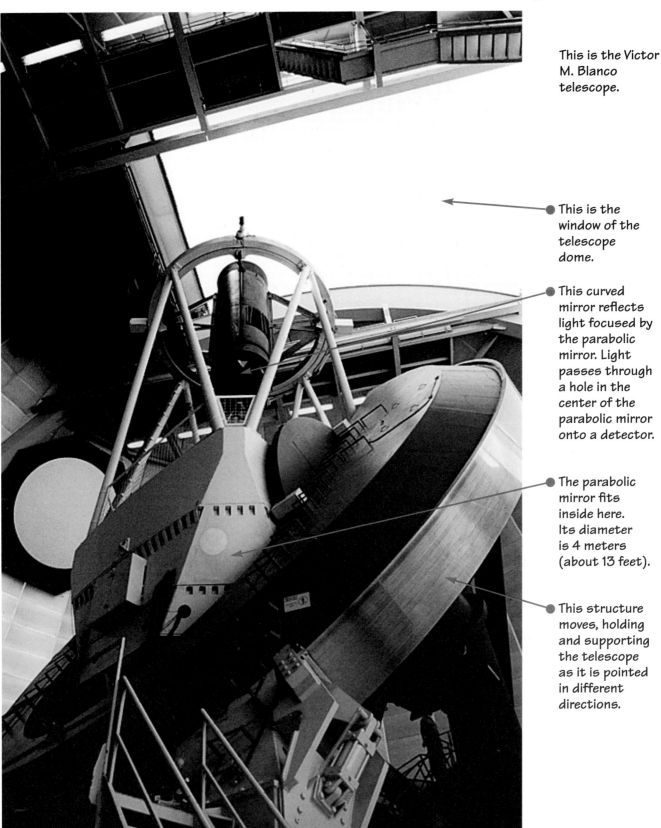

This is the Victor M. Blanco telescope.

● This is the window of the telescope dome.

● This curved mirror reflects light focused by the parabolic mirror. Light passes through a hole in the center of the parabolic mirror onto a detector.

● The parabolic mirror fits inside here. Its diameter is 4 meters (about 13 feet).

● This structure moves, holding and supporting the telescope as it is pointed in different directions.

list were too far away for me to see their dust disks. But a star with a dust disk appears brighter in infrared light than the same star would appear without a disk. I planned to look for this extra infrared light. The committee approved my proposal. So several months later, on a March night in 1998, I was on a mountain in Chile. I had been given four nights to use the telescope at the CTIO.

Hunting Disks

My first night at CTIO was completely cloudy. You couldn't even see the moon, much less faint stars. A cloudy night sky is an astronomer's nightmare. When you come to a place like CTIO, you have only the nights that you have been assigned by the committee. You don't get extra time if the weather is bad. There's little to do but sit, wait, and hope the weather improves. Sometimes you just watch a video, or read a book and eat your "night lunch."

Charles (Charlie) Telesco and Scott Fisher were also in the control room with Patricio (Pato) Ugarte, the Chilean telescope operator, and me. Charlie is an astronomy professor at the University of Florida. Scott is one of his students. Charlie built the camera that we would use to take infrared pictures. His team filled eight crates with the camera, cables, and computers. Then he shipped them all the way from Florida.

The camera is attached to the back end of the telescope. The pictures appear on a computer screen inside a control room. The telescope and camera can be adjusted with commands from the computer.

Around 4:00 A.M., there was no sign that the clouds would part, so we quit for the night. We drove down the mountain to the observatory's dormitory and went to bed. This was not a happy way to begin my work.

The next night, most of the clouds had cleared. But

Astronomer Charlie Telesco is attaching the infrared camera that he built to the back end of the telescope.

the air was too humid. I pointed the telescope at a few of my "target stars," the stars on my list. But the weather made it hard for me to get a good view of these stars.

The third night was much better. We took pictures of three more stars. But there were no signs of disks. Around 1:00 A.M., I decided to point the telescope at HR 4796A, a ten-million-year-old star. Many astronomers thought it might have a dust disk. We took pictures of the star using one filter. A filter is a device that lets light in only a certain band of wavelengths into the camera.

HR 4796A looked bright in the pictures, but we didn't see a disk. Then we looked at the star with a different filter. The new filter let infrared light with longer wavelengths into the camera. To look for faint images, we left the camera shutters open longer to let in more light. After about 20 minutes, we noticed that the picture forming on the computer screen connected to the camera seemed to be long and narrow instead of pointed like a star. "Are we seeing a dust disk?" we wondered aloud.

Scott (seated) and I are watching the computer as it receives the image of disk HR 4796A. A disk is very dim, so a camera's shutters must stay open longer to collect more light. That means it takes some time for pictures to develop on the screen.

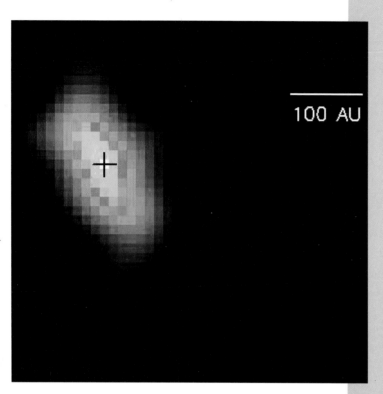

100 AU

Separation of Infrared Light

Infrared light is the name given in the wave model of light to light that covers a certain range of wavelengths. Scientists are often concerned with only one part of this range at a time. For that reason, scientists separate the infrared into three parts. They are called near-, mid-, and far-infrared light.

Earth's atmosphere affects how much infrared light reaches telescopes on the ground. Near-infrared light passes through easily. Water vapor in our atmosphere partly absorbs mid-infrared light. It can be detected with some difficulty by telescopes built on dry mountaintops. Our atmosphere blocks far-infrared light entirely. It can only be detected from space.

The dust around adolescent stars shines with mostly far-infrared and mid-infrared light. There are no big telescopes in space now that can detect far-infrared light. So we took pictures in mid-infrared light from a telescope on the ground. Astronomers often use false colors in making pictures of stars. Colors can clearly show the differences in the amount of light coming from different regions in the sky. We used false colors in this picture.

The disk around HR 4796A was confirmed by the picture above. The "+" marks the location of the star. The line and "100 AU" are used to measure distance, like a scale on a road map. "AU" stands for "Astronomical Unit." An AU is the average distance between Earth and the sun, so the length of the line is equal to 100 times this average distance.

I was afraid it was too good to be true. I asked Scott if the telescope could be out of focus. He was sure it was not. Charlie, who has had more experience than I with infrared cameras, was also sure the picture was real.

Once the picture was complete, we looked at a different star. We wanted to be sure the focus was right. It was. Now we knew that we had discovered a dust disk around a ten-million-year-old star. We were thrilled. Charlie was almost dancing. "This is a big discovery. This is huge!" he exclaimed.

We took more pictures of HR 4796A until dawn. We wanted more evidence to convince other astronomers that we had found an adolescent star with a disk. By the time the sun rose, we were tired but still excited. Scott and I stayed up two more hours to study the images.

Then we sent them to my professors at the CfA. We wanted someone else to confirm our discovery. We had to be sure we hadn't made a mistake. They agreed we had found what we were looking for. A week later I went to Florida to study the images again with Scott. We measured the disk's size and brightness precisely.

As we prepared to announce our big discovery, we learned that another team of astronomers had taken a picture of the same disk at almost exactly the same time. They used a telescope in Hawaii the same week we were in Chile. Both teams received credit for the discovery.

Why did the two teams find the disk at almost the same time? The answer includes technology and chance. Improved infrared cameras had just become available. Before then, this discovery wasn't possible. Many astronomers wanted to use the new cameras, and HR 4796A was a good target for disk hunting. But why the same week? It was simply a coincidence that both teams' observations were scheduled for the same time.

Here I am with Charlie (background) and Scott, pointing to the image of the disk we discovered.

5

FROM DUST TO PLANETS

"We think that the dust material around HR 4796A has formed a disk that is three times as large as our own solar system. The hole we see in its center may in fact have been cleared by a planet, but we can't see it directly."—Charles Telesco

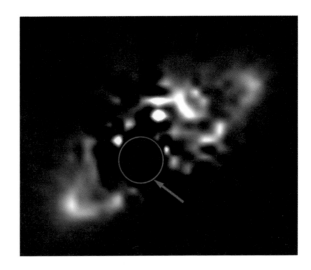

The discovery of a disk around HR 4796A was exciting. It was just the type of snapshot astronomers needed. We knew about dark clouds from William Herschel. We had pictures of dark clouds and pictures of cores. We had pictures of young stars with disks and mature stars with little or no disks. But we didn't have a picture of a "teenage" star with a disk. At about ten million years old, HR 4796A is just the right age for planets to be forming. The discovery gives us another piece of evidence to help develop a good model of how planets form. For more evidence, it would help to have pictures of disks around stars of other ages. These could show planetary systems at various stages of development.

Astronomers already have some evidence about how planets form. The disks observed around the baby stars in Orion tell us that young disks have huge amounts of gas and dust. These are the materials for making planets. We also know that the disk around star HR 4796A has much less gas and dust than are found in disks that revolve around younger stars.

We have since found that HR 4796A's disk has a hole in its middle. Perhaps dust that was once in the inner part of the disk is now part of a planet. That would

(above)
This is an image of the HR 4796A disk obtained by the Hubble Space Telescope. A round spot placed on the camera blocks the star's light. Blocking the star's light makes it possible to see the disk.

(left)
This painting shows a disk in which planets are starting to form. We can't see stars and their disks in great detail. But we can use models of star formation to make an educated guess as to how such faraway objects might look.

43

explain the hole. But we can't be sure, because we can't directly see any planets around HR 4796A. However, there are clues.

Clues come in many forms. They even fall from the sky. Astronomers believe comets and asteroids are material left over after the planets in our solar system formed. They can tell researchers a lot about those early days.

Comets are icy dust balls. They are from the outer solar system, beyond Jupiter. Scientists think they are made of the same materials as are in the cores of giant planets like Jupiter and Saturn.

Asteroids are chunks of rock usually from the inner solar system. They are probably made of material like the material on rocky planets, such as Earth and Mars. There are many thousands of asteroids between the orbits of Mars and Jupiter. Those asteroids might be

Astronomers study comets like Hale-Bopp, shown below, to find more clues about what the early days of the solar system were like. The ground in this photograph appears curved because the photographer used a fisheye lens.

bodies that never came together to form a planet.

Over the past 15 years, several space probes have been sent to study comets and asteroids. There are also plans for space missions to return with samples of comet and asteroid material for study on Earth.

But scientists already have samples from the early solar system in their laboratories. These samples are called meteorites. Meteorites are pieces of asteroids or comets that fall to Earth. Usually they burn up as they move through Earth's atmosphere. They appear as shooting stars, or meteors. Sometimes a piece of an asteroid or comet does not burn completely. A part survives to reach the ground. Such a part is called a meteorite. Scientists study meteorites to learn what they're made of. This knowledge helps them find out what materials were in the disk that once spun around our young sun. Such evidence can help astronomers understand how the planets in our solar system formed.

Making a Planet

Scientists can combine what they've learned from observing disks and studying meteorites to create computer models of how planets might form. The models start with little grains of dust and particles of gas. When the dust grains collide at slow enough speeds, they tend to stick together. When enough grains stick together, they can become objects as large as pebbles. When pebbles collide, they could stick together, too. This process could lead to the formation of kilometer-sized objects called "planetesimals."

But in the models astronomers have developed so far, pebbles do not stick together to form planetesimals very easily. So for now, this part of the process of planet formation remains a mystery. Of course, we may not have a

This is a slice of the Kapoeta meteorite, found in Sudan in eastern Africa. The meteorite is believed to have come from an asteroid called 4 Vesta. The Kapoeta meteorite weighs about 11 kilograms (about 24 pounds). This piece weighs about 2 grams (about .07 ounce).

useful model to explain how planets form, but nature knows how to form planets. Our own planetary system is the evidence.

Although their models of planet formation remain uncertain, scientists think that after a few million years, rocky planets like Earth and Mars form. Their models also tell them that gaseous planets need more time to form. At large enough distances from a star, it is cold enough for ice to form in the disk. Ice provides a lot of material for making planets. In our solar system, gaseous planets like Jupiter and Saturn are far enough from the sun for ice to form. Scientists believe that these planets first formed cores ten times the mass of Earth. With such massive cores, these planets could continue to grow by sweeping up enough gas to form their huge atmospheres.

But collecting so much gas is thought to be a slow process. Some computer models show this process could take ten million years or more. That puzzles some astronomers. Young stars often produce strong winds.

Asteroids are believed to be leftovers from planet-making and may have changed very little from the time our solar system was formed. So, scientists believe that they may learn more about that time by studying asteroids like Ida (above) and Gaspara (right). Both orbit between Mars and Jupiter. Scientists estimate that Ida is about 52 kilometers (about 32 miles) in length, and that Gaspara is about half Ida's length. The two asteroids were photographed by NASA's Galileo spacecraft as it traveled from Earth to Jupiter.

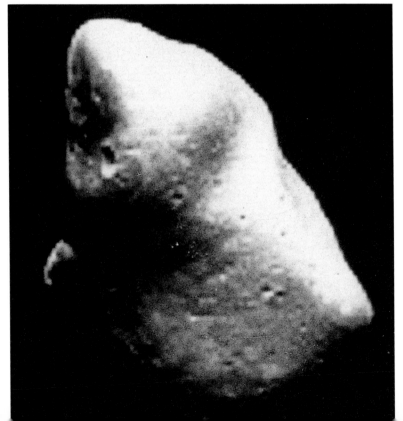

Planet formation models include information gathered by devices such as NASA's Galileo spacecraft. The Galileo spacecraft is shown in this artist's picture. The spacecraft would actually look like a very, very tiny speck compared with the size of Jupiter.

Could Jupiter and Saturn have collected the huge amount of gas in their atmospheres before winds from our sun blew the gas away? Or is there another model for the formation of gaseous planets that solves the problem? We astronomers don't know, but we're working to find out.

Developing a model that describes how a planetary system forms isn't easy, even with the help of computers. We need more clues from nature. Do the dust disks that we see around other stars turn into planets? Recent discoveries suggest that they do.

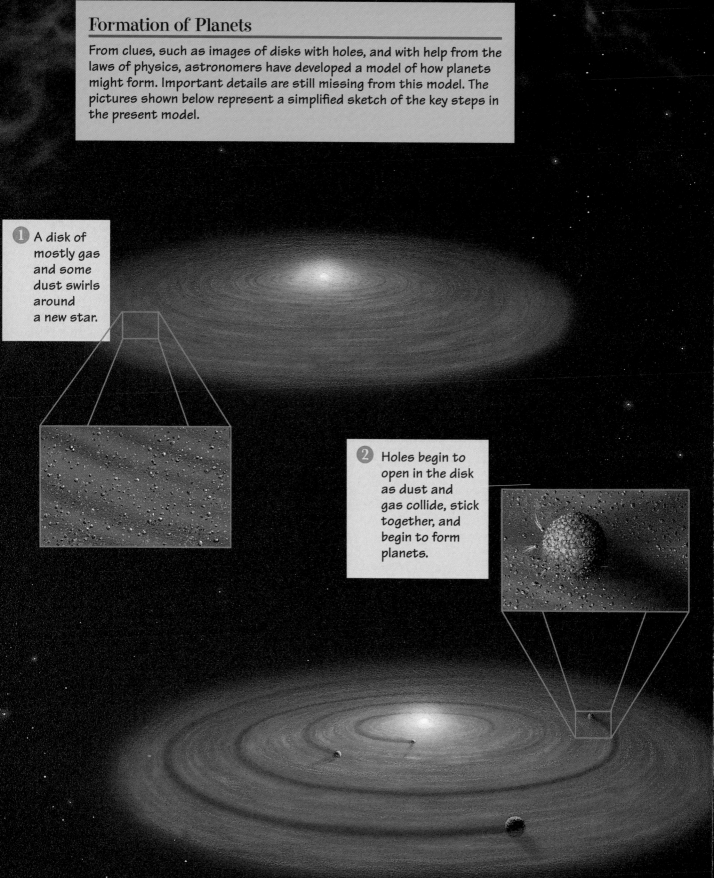

Formation of Planets

From clues, such as images of disks with holes, and with help from the laws of physics, astronomers have developed a model of how planets might form. Important details are still missing from this model. The pictures shown below represent a simplified sketch of the key steps in the present model.

1 A disk of mostly gas and some dust swirls around a new star.

2 Holes begin to open in the disk as dust and gas collide, stick together, and begin to form planets.

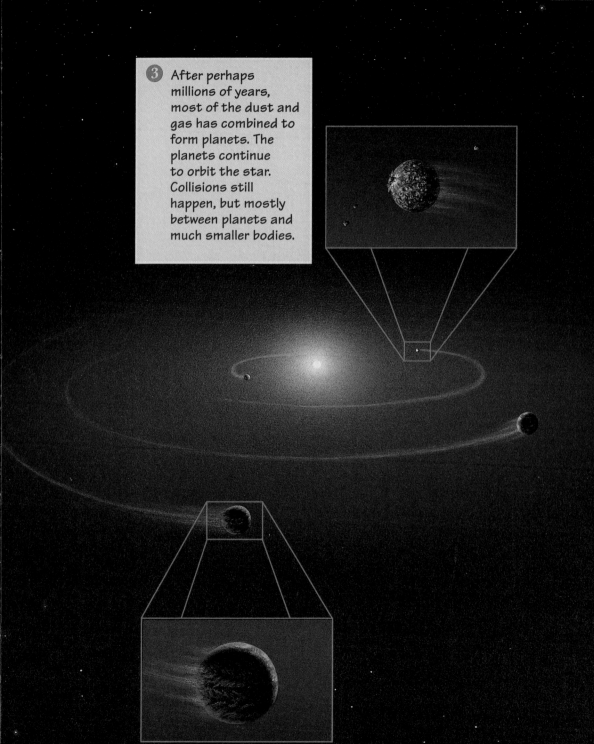

3 After perhaps millions of years, most of the dust and gas has combined to form planets. The planets continue to orbit the star. Collisions still happen, but mostly between planets and much smaller bodies.

Moon-Making

There have been many models developed to explain how the moon was made. George Darwin, the son of scientist Charles Darwin, proposed a model in 1878. He suggested that the moon is a piece of Earth, thrown off as Earth rotated very, very fast in its early days. But Harvard-Smithsonian scientist Alastair "Al" Cameron pointed out that for this model to be correct, "both Earth and the moon would have to be spinning much faster than they do."

Another model suggests that the moon formed in the same way that other planets did. "If that happened, the moon and the planets would have about the same percentage of metallic iron in their bodies," Al explains. But the moon's core seems to have far less iron.

A third model suggests that the moon formed somewhere else and was captured by Earth's gravitational pull as it passed by Earth. Al has calculated that it is almost impossible for this to have happened. It is far more likely that the moon would have hit Earth or been lost in space.

In the 1970s, Al and another scientist, William Ward, came up with a new idea. Their model was that the moon formed from material left by a collision between Earth and a planet the size of Mars. To test this theory, dozens of computer models have been made. In each model, the other planet was destroyed, and water vapor and bits of rock shot into Earth's orbit.

These models began with different conditions, such as the size of the other planet and the speed at which it hit Earth. But all the models ended with a disk of material circling Earth. How could that material have formed the moon? Robin Canup (below) of the Southwest Research Institute in Boulder, Colorado, set out to answer that question. In 1997 she and fellow scientists presented their first models.

Their computer models showed that the particles in the disk clumped together to form one or two moons. Each model began with different starting conditions, such as different numbers and sizes of the particles. But at least one moon formed every time. One-third of the time, two moons formed instead of one. "That would have been quite a sight," Robin notes. But two moons would grace Earth's sky for only a short time. In every model either one moon crashed into Earth or the two moons collided.

At the time of its birth, the moon was much closer to Earth than it is today. Robin's models indicate that the moon formed about 22,000 kilometers (about 14,000 miles) from Earth's surface. Now it orbits Earth at an average distance of 380,000 kilometers (about 240,000 miles). Robin's models also suggest that during the first few hundred million years after it formed, the moon moved out to about half its present distance from Earth. The moon is still moving away, but slowly. It moves less than 4 centimeters (about 1 ½ inches) each year.

6
OTHER WORLDS

"Earthlike planets will be harder to detect because they are much smaller than giant planets like Jupiter, but it should be possible to detect them from space. Such missions are now under study."
—Dave Latham, CfA

For centuries scientists knew of the existence of only one planetary system—our own. They have wondered if other planets existed outside our solar system. Until recently we didn't know for sure. But there is now evidence that planets revolve around many nearby stars.

In the same week that the two teams announced the discovery of the HR 4796A disk, another team of astronomers in Hawaii announced a different discovery. They reported seeing disks around three mature stars. They found the disks by using a telescope that could detect radio waves emitted by dust particles. The team, led by Jane Greaves and Wayne Holland of the Joint Astronomy Center in Hilo, Hawaii, took pictures of disks around the stars Beta Pictoris, Vega, and Fomalhaut. These stars are somewhat older than HR 4796A, but they are still much younger than our five-billion-year-old sun.

A few months later, Jane and Wayne also took a picture of a fourth star, Epsilon Eridani. This star is closer to Earth than the other three, so they could see more details. What they saw looked like what they expected comets in our outer solar system would look like if they were viewed from the distance of Epsilon Eridani.

(above)
Wayne Holland and Jane Greaves hunt for disks using a radio telescope in Hawaii.

(left)
In this artist's painting, a giant planet bigger than Jupiter orbits very close to its star.

Dust disks with holes and bright spots may be new planetary systems in the making. If so, some must be already made, with fully formed planets. Finding those planets would support the theory that dust disks evolve into planetary systems. But the planets are hard to see through the glare of the planets' stars. Nonetheless, astronomers are close to being able to detect them.

Recently, astronomers' instruments have been able to detect stars whose distances from Earth change periodically. These movements signal the presence of planets. Instruments can now detect this motion only when there is a large planet close to the parent star. In this way, astronomers have found planets in orbit around at least 30 grown-up stars.

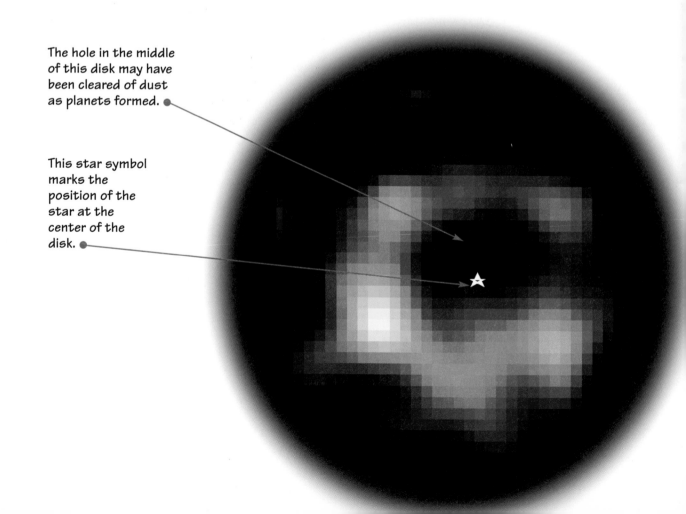

This image of the Epsilon Eridani disk shows a hole in the middle. The entire disk is about 1,300 light-minutes across. This disk is positioned in the sky so that we see it "face on."

The hole in the middle of this disk may have been cleared of dust as planets formed.

This star symbol marks the position of the star at the center of the disk.

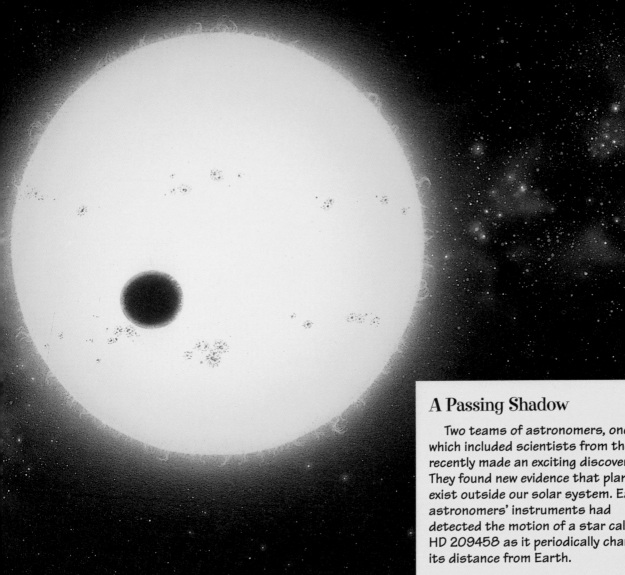

Only planets as big as or bigger than Jupiter have been found by measuring these motions. And most of these planets are much closer to their parent star than astronomers had predicted. Some are much closer than Mercury is to our sun. How can a planet larger than Jupiter be so close to its star? Astronomers are debating the answer to this question. Whatever the answer turns out to be, these discoveries show that other solar systems can be quite different from our own.

A Passing Shadow

Two teams of astronomers, one of which included scientists from the CfA, recently made an exciting discovery. They found new evidence that planets exist outside our solar system. Earlier, astronomers' instruments had detected the motion of a star called HD 209458 as it periodically changed its distance from Earth.

Then in 1999 the astronomers turned another telescope to HD 209458. For about two hours, they observed a decrease in the star's brightness. This was followed by a similar increase in brightness. The same pattern was observed again, as expected, one week later. This dimming was the effect of a planet's shadow passing in front of the star as we view it from Earth. With observations like these, astronomers can determine such information as the density of the planet, and can even study its atmosphere. Above is an artist's picture of star HD 209458 and its passing planet.

The Space InfraRed Telescope Facility (SIRTF) will be a very powerful infrared telescope that will orbit the sun and detect infrared light from objects in space. NASA plans to launch SIRTF in December 2001.

Primary mirror

Star tracker

Helium tank

Housing for electronics for telescope camera

Astronomers are working to develop a model of how a giant planet that is so close to its parent star could have formed. The best idea so far is that the planet forms far from the star. Then it moves closer. But by what process does it move closer? Is this process common? In our solar system, only small planets orbit close to the sun. The giant planets orbit much farther away. Is our solar system unusual? Astronomers just don't know.

Each new discovery seems to raise new questions. Astronomers use new instruments to try to answer these questions. Before too long, a new generation of observatories on the ground and in space may help scientists add to the story of how stars and planets are born.

Among the most exciting new observatories is a spacecraft called the Space InfraRed Telescope Facility (SIRTF). It is being built by NASA and will orbit the sun. One reason SIRTF will orbit the sun rather than Earth is that Earth emits infrared light. This light can make it harder for a spacecraft in orbit around Earth to detect distant, faint objects. Also, satellites that orbit Earth can't record images when Earth is between the satellites and the objects they are observing. "The solar orbit allows us to observe without being disturbed by Earth's infrared glow," says Giovanni Fazio, an astronomer at the CfA. Giovanni leads a team that is building one of the three main instruments that will be carried onboard SIRTF.

SIRTF's advanced technology and solar orbit will make SIRTF far more powerful than other satellites that make observations in infrared light. It will be able to take pictures of disks around nearby stars. With SIRTF, we should be able to find out what the disks are made of and look for holes in them. SIRTF will also look for dust disks around thousands of more distant stars to find out how common disks may be.

New technology will be used to improve ground-based telescopes, too. For example, it is now possible to combine the light from two or more ground-based infrared telescopes. This technique allows astronomers to see finer details than they can see using individual telescopes. Very soon, scientists hope to combine light from the two 10-meter (about 30-foot) diameter Keck telescopes in Hawaii. In northern Chile, four 8-meter European telescopes grouped together are called the Very Large Telescope (VLT). Their images will also be combined so that finer details can be observed.

Scientists are continually developing new technologies and techniques to help them see more of the universe and uncover more of its secrets. Over the past 20 years, astronomers have learned much about the origin of stars

The Very Large Telescope (VLT), on top of a mountain in northern Chile, is composed of four separate telescopes. They will make observations of the sky in visible and infrared light.

Picture This

The Harvard-Smithsonian Center for Astrophysics, together with Taiwan's Institute for Astronomy and Astrophysics, is building an array of eight radio telescopes on top of Mauna Kea, an inactive volcano in Hawaii.

The Submillimeter Array (SMA) will be able to detect "submillimeter waves." These are waves with lengths less than 1 millimeter (about .04 inch). Submillimeter waves are emitted by cold dust around nearby stars.

By combining the signals from all eight telescopes, the SMA will make pictures of disks in greater detail than ever before. SMA images may show the holes that newborn planets should, according to our models, create in disks.

and planets. We have used instruments that detect infrared light to look deep into star factories. There, we have been able to see newborn stars that are hidden by dust and gas when viewed in visible light.

Astronomers have also studied spectacular pictures of young stars circled by dust disks, the possible beginnings of planetary systems. Images of some disks around adolescent stars have shown evidence, such as holes and bright spots, of planets. And many mature stars have planets that orbit around them. But the story is far from complete. Many important questions remain. How common are planetary systems? Are any of them like our solar system? Could there be life on other planets? The search continues.

With new telescopes and new ways of using them, astronomers hope to learn more of the universe's secrets, including the birth of stars and planets.

GLOSSARY

asteroid [AZ-ter-oyd] Chunks of rock that range in length from smaller than a meter to several hundred kilometers in length. There are many asteroids in orbit around the sun, mostly between the orbits of Mars and Jupiter.

astronomers Scientists who study the whole universe, including its origin and the nature and behavior of objects in outer space.

atmosphere Gases around a star or planet, such as Earth.

atom The smallest known unit of any particular kind of matter.

comet A chunk of frozen gases, water, dirt, and rock that orbits the sun. Comets are various sizes.

constellation A set of stars in the sky that forms a recognizable pattern in peoples' imaginations.

density The amount of matter in a specific quantity of space.

galaxy A large collection of stars that can be seen in the sky. Our sun and its planets are in the Milky Way galaxy.

gamma rays Light that we cannot see with our eyes. In the wave model of light, gamma rays have the shortest wavelengths.

gas The state of matter in which molecules can be far apart from one another and move about independently. A gas has no definite shape. Gas spreads out to fill any container it is in. Other states of matter are solid and liquid. A solid has a definite shape, and a liquid takes the shape of its container, but may not fill it.

giant molecular cloud A large cloud of gas and dust where it is thought new stars are made. Such a cloud is often composed of about 99 percent gas and 1 percent dust.

infrared light Light that we cannot see with our eyes. According to the wave model of light, infrared light has longer wavelengths than visible light.

laws of physics Models of nature's behavior that seem to hold true everywhere on Earth and also everywhere in the universe.

Milky Way galaxy The galaxy that contains our solar system. To the unaided eye, the Milky Way appears as a faint band of light in the night sky.

model A theory based on observations of nature's behavior. Models can be used to predict future outcomes.

molecular cloud [see giant molecular cloud]

nebula [NEH-byoo-lah] A cloud of dust and gas that appears as a dim or dark region in the sky, depending on whether the nebula reflects or blocks light from stars.

parabolic mirror [pair-uh-BOHL-ick] One of the mirrors inside a reflecting telescope. Inside the telescope, light travels parallel to the sides of the tube. The light is reflected by the mirror toward a single point, called the focus.

radio waves Light that we cannot see with our eyes. In the wave model of light, radio waves have longer wavelengths than infrared light.

satellite A natural or human-made object in space that moves in orbit around a planet.

space probe A spacecraft with instruments used to gather information about outer space. A space probe's fuel allows it to reach a high enough velocity to travel far from Earth.

spectrum For light visible to human eyes, a spectrum is the distribution of colors, from red to blue, that we see—for example, when sunlight passes through a prism.

ultraviolet light Light that we cannot see with our eyes. According to the wave model of light, ultraviolet light has shorter wavelengths than visible light.

visible light Light that we can see with our eyes.

wavelength Light can be modelled as waves. A wavelength is the distance from any part of a wave to the same part of the next (or previous) wave.

X-rays Light that we cannot see with our eyes. According to the wave model of light, X-rays have shorter wavelengths than ultraviolet light, and longer wavelengths than gamma rays.

FURTHER READING

Atkinson, Stuart. *Usborne Understanding Science: Astronomy.* Tulsa, OK: Education Development Center Publishing, 1998.

Couper, Heather and Nigel Henbest. *Big Bang: The Story of the Universe.* New York, NY: DK Publishing, 1997.

Dickinson, Terrence. *Exploring the Night Sky.* Buffalo, NY: Firefly Books, 1998.

Ford, Harry. *The Young Astronomer.* London: Dorling Kindersley Publishing, 1998.

National Wildlife Federation. *Ranger Rick's Nature Scope: Astronomy Adventures.* New York, NY: McGraw Hill, 1997.

The New York Public Library. *Amazing Space: A Book of Answers for Kids.* New York, NY: John Wiley & Sons, 1997.

Rey, H. A. *The Stars: A New Way to See Them.* Boston, MA: Houghton Mifflin Co., 1976.

Ridpath, Ian, et al. *Eyewitness Handbooks: Stars and Planets.* New York, NY: DK Publishing, 1998.

VanCleave, Janice. *Janice VanCleave's Constellations for Every Kid.* New York: John Wiley, 1997.

INDEX

Acknowledgments

The author would like to thank Irwin Shapiro for a thorough review of the book and Matthew Schneps and Debbie Kovacs for asking him to write it. The author is also indebted to scientists who provided interviews, information, and illustrations.

Benson, Patricia, courtesy of: 21 top left and bottom right; Boden/Ledingham, Masterfile: 13 top; Brandner, Wolfgang/JPL and IPAC, Eva K. Grebel/University of Washington, You-Hua Chu/University of Illinois Urbana-Champaign, National Aeronautics and Space Administration (NASA): 1 background; Burrows, Chris/Space Telescope Science Institute (STScI), WFPC2 Science Team, NASA: 29 main image; Caltech Institute Archives: 27; Casado, J.C.: 44; Compton Gamma Ray Observatory: 16 left, second from top; Credner, T. and S. Kohl/Calar Alto Observatory: 2 left; Digel, Seth, Compton Observatory Science Support Center, NASA/GSFC: 16 top left; European Southern Observatory: 4, 18 top left, 57; Figer, Don, STScI, NASA: 12; Finley, David, National Radio Astronomy Observatory/Associated Universities, Inc.: 17 two upper right images; Greaves, Jane and Wayne Holland, courtesy of: 53, 54; Hubble Space Telescope/NASA: 43; Hurley, Jim: 45; Infrared Processing and Analysis Center (IPAC)/Caltech: 18 bottom left; Jayawardhana, Ray, *Muse* Magazine: 41; Jayawardhana, Ray/CfA, Lee Hartmann/CfA, Giovanni Fazio/CfA, Scott Fisher/University of Florida, Gainsville, Charles Telesco/UF, Robert Pina/UF, Cerro Tololo Inter-American Observatory, La Serena, Chile: 40; Johnson Space Center: 9 upper right, 29 upper right; JPL Picture Archive: 47; Lada, Charles, courtesy of: 20; Lada, Elizabeth/UF: 18 bottom right, 25; Malin, David, Anglo Australian Observatory: 11, 17 two upper left images; Max Planck Institute: 16 two bottom images; McDonald, Kim: 2 right, 3, 19, 36, 37, 38, 39; McCaughrean, M.J./Max Planck Institute for Astronomy C.R. O'Dell/Rice University, NASA: 2 middle, 26; McNally, Joseph: 1 inset, cover inset; NASA: 46, 50–51; NASA/Beyond the Blue, Greatest Hits of the Ultraviolet Imaging Telescope: 16 two upper right images; NASA/National Space Science Data Center, The Hubble Space Telescope: 8; Nowitz, Richard: 24; O'Dell, C.R./Rice University, NASA: 9 bottom; Padgett, D./IPAC/Caltech: 28; Palomar Observatory/Caltech: 17 bottom right; Palomar Observatory/Caltech, Danner/Hogg: 7, 17 bottom right; Royal Astronomical Society, London: 5, 6 bottom left; Simpson, Elisabeth, 1996/FPG International/LLC: 15; Smith, Bradford A./University of Hawaii, Richard J. Terrile/JPL: 32, 33; Smith, R. Chris/University of Michigan, Cerro Tololo Inter-American Observatory, National Optical Astronomy Observatories: 30; Smith, Roger, NOAO/NSF at the Association of Universities for Research in Astronomy, all rights reserved: 34; Solar and Heliospheric Observatory: 10, 31; Space Infrared Telescope Facility: 56; Submillimeter Array, Mauna Kea: 59; Tedds, Jonathan/University of Leeds: 21 top right; Wiltse, John: 51 inset; Wiseman, Jennifer/STScI: 21 middle.

Illustration on page 6 is by David Griffin. Illustrations on pages 22–23, 42, 48–49, 52, 55, and 59 are by Lynette Cook. Illustration on page 35 is by Jill Leichter.